CAPITAL AS POWER

A CONCISE SUMMARY OF THE MARXIST ANALYSIS OF CAPITALISM

BY

JORN K. BRAMANN

ADLER PUBLISHING COMPANY
Rochester, New York

CAPITAL AS POWER
A Concise Summary of The Marxist Analysis of Capitalism

TO LYN AND ALAN IN FRIENDSHIP

First Edition

Copyright © 1984 by Jorn K. Bramann.

For information address
Adler Publishing Company
P.O. Box 9342
Rochester, N.Y. 14604

Illustrations by Kathleen Kaminski

Cover Design by Sasha Trouslot / Foxglove Graphics, Inc.

ISBN 0-913623-04-0
Library of Congress Catalog Card Number: 84-71438
Printed in the United States of America

89 88 87 86 85 84   5 4 3 2 1

CONTENTS

"I have been on the Board for a quarter of a century,
and I have yet to see an *excess* profit!"

PREFACE

The following is a presentation of the basic features of capitalist societies as seen from a Marxist point of view. This presentation grew out of the task of conveying the basic concepts of Marxism to students who had never encountered these concepts in a serious and coherent fashion. It is designed for readers who do not have the time, inclination, opportunity, or patience to read through a certain amount of Marxist literature, but who could benefit in one way or another from a concise summary of the Marxist analysis of Capitalism.

What primarily distinguishes a Marxist analysis of Capitalism from other kinds is the fact that Marxists see Capital not only as an economic entity, but as a social force in the broadest sense. In the eyes of Marxists, Capital figures not only in the production and distribution of goods, but also in the formation of social organizations, legal structures, political activities, individual behavior, and a good deal of a society's intellectual culture. For this reason, the following presentation is centered around the active role which Capital plays in its own reproduction, as well as in other human affairs: it describes Capital as power.

Another reason for describing Capital as power is the inherent tendency of Capital to constantly increase its rule over human affairs. Many products of human culture, such as customs, laws, governments, cities, or the market, not only develop a life of their own, but also shape and influence the life of their makers. Cities are the products of people, but people are in many ways also the products of cities. "But lo! men have become the tools of their tools," Thoreau once remarked in *Walden*. And this reversal of efficacy has become particularly dramatic in the case of Capital. The development of Capital from its humble origins as the surplus of human production to its powerful role as prime motivator of all decisive human enterprises is therefore at the heart of the Marxist analysis of capitalism.

Capital As Power follows this development, the first part concentrating on the more narrowly economic aspects, the second part explaining some of the major social implications of the growth of Capital. It begins with the simple fact that most working people produce more than they need for their mere survival, and the additional fact that most of this surplus accrues to those who own the means of production. It ends with the situation in which societies are driven by the seemingly inexorable need to desperately search for ever new investment opportunities, raw material sources, energy and markets in which the ever more voluminous cycle of production and consumption has become the overriding purpose of life, in which limitless industrialization seriously threatens the environment in which people have to live, and in which, nevertheless, governments are powerless to check the polarization of the Western World's population into an affluent minority, and the growing mass of the poor. It tries to present the above development in such a way that its steps can be seen to follow plausibly from each other, that today's situation is recognizable as the logical conclusion of the initial premises of capitalist production. *Capital As Power*, in other words, tries to show how the various aspects and phases of Capitalism hang together, and how they are bound to evolve in a predictable way (unless they are consciously interfered with). It tries to depict the inner logic of Capital.

Due to presenting only the most basic features of Capitalism, *Capital As Power* does not discuss a number of important issues which would have to be included in a more extensive description of capitalist societies. Such issues are the power of banks as controllers of credit, the special role of women in the workforce and as sustainers of that workforce, or the discrimination against ethnic minorities. Passing over these topics does not mean that their discussion is unimportant for the understanding of contemporary society, but only that they are not essential for understanding the basic features of Capitalism. Racism, e.g., can exist independently of Capitalism, and Capitalism can function perfectly well without racism (cf. also Part II, Chapter 1). That racism under certain circumstances works to the advantage of capitalist entrepreneurs is a result of the fact that Capitalism developed under a number of special historical and geographical conditions. *Capital As Power* is confined to dealing with those features which are common to *all* forms of Capitalism.

I sincerely thank Arthur Axelrod, Jeanette Axelrod, and John Moran for their criticism and kind help in preparing this summary.

Little Savage Mountain, Maryland
Fall, 1983

"Gentlemen, you *can* fight an idea whose time has come!"

THE DEVELOPMENT OF CAPITAL

THE CREATION OF SURPLUS VALUE

A craftsman (a shoemaker, for example) who owns his own shop can, under certain circumstances, make a living by working for himself. His working hours can be divided in the following way: First he has to work long enough to take care of his means of subsistence such as food, shelter, clothing and other necessities. He may have to work 4 hours every day to produce enough shoes to earn $16, which, when sold, will take care of these items. After this he will have to work for an additional period of time to pay for his means of production, such as shop and equipment, raw materials, energy, and overhead. This may amount to one hour of work per day, or to a value of $4. (These figures are, of course, arbitrary. It should also be noticed that all quantities mentioned are averages. Obviously there are craftsmen with and without families, fast workers and slow ones, persons who are parsimonious and persons who are wasteful, etc. Such individual differences are, however, irrelevant for the analysis of the basic patterns of economic relations).

After 5 hours the craftsman is free to quit work, as he has produced enough of everything which is necessary for the survival of himself and his shop. If he continues to work, however, he will have extra money, and he will have all the more extra money the longer he extends his working day beyond the first 5 hours. If he works 8 hours per day he will, in terms of the above example, have a daily surplus of $12. Let the value produced during the time after the first 5 hours be called "surplus value." It is this "surplus value" which is the inner core of Capitalism and its development, and to understand the power of Capital is tantamount to understanding the role and evolution of "surplus value." In a graphical representation, "surplus value" can be depicted as follows:

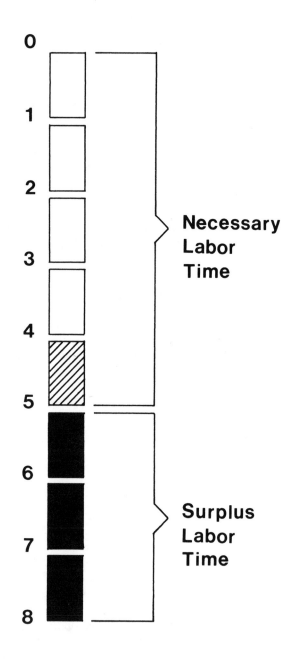

THE OWNERSHIP OF SURPLUS VALUE

In a case where the craftsman and the owner of the shop are two different persons, everything remains the same — except for the ownership of surplus value. The craftsman is required by contract to work for 8 hours every day (the legal length of the working day). In these 8 hours he produces (in terms of the above example) merchandise valued at $32. His subsistence requires that he be paid at least $16 in wages. Another $4 goes toward paying for the means of production. The remaining $12, however, the surplus value of the goods that he has produced, are the gain of the shop owner; they are his gross profit. The owner is entitled to this profit because he owns the means of production, and because he has paid for the labor power which he uses in the process of production.

(It is irrelevant whether owners of means of production work themselves or not: their profits accrue to them not because they work, if they do, but because they own. Many owners do, in fact, work. But their profits are not based on the amount of work they do, but on the extent of their holdings. An owner of several factories, whose income is a quarter of a million dollars a year, cannot possibly work 250 times as hard as any one of his workers earning $25,000 in the same time).

It is clear that the owner of the shop could not allow his hired craftsman to quit work after 5 hours. If he did, the produced value per day would be just $20, the sum which is necessary to maintain the craftsman and the shop. The owner would not derive any benefit from owning the shop, and thus would have no incentive for acquiring it in the first place. The owner has to insist that the craftsman give at least a minimal amount of what is called "surplus labor time."

It is also clear that under most circumstances it would be more advantageous for the craftsman to work for himself; not only because it is more agreeable to work at one's own pace, and to make one's own decisions, but because one could then collect the surplus value oneself. The reason why most people do not work for themselves is that they do not own sufficient means of production. Because of this, they are forced to sell their labor power to someone who does. Since the vast majority of people in modern capitalist societies do not own sufficient means of production, these societies are characterized by the fact that the majority of their members are dependent for their livlihood on the employment by a minority of owners.

Owners of means of production are in a position to buy the labor power of other people because they can use it profitably. They can use it in such a way that they can get more out of it than it costs them. In terms of the above example, it would cost the owner $16 a day to buy a worker's labor power. But this labor power produces a total value of $32 during the 8 hours of the working day, leaving the owner (after subtracting wages and payment for the means of production) with a surplus value of $12. Labor power, in other words, has the fortunate characteristic of producing more value than it costs itself. This use of labor power constitutes the technical sense of "exploitation" of labor power: owners of means of production are said to "exploit" workers because they use the workers' labor power to create surplus value for themselves.

(It should be noticed that owners do not have to run a "sweat shop" to be "exploiters" in this sense. Owners who pay their workers above average wages, and who treat them kindly, still "exploit" them by virtue of appropriating the produced surplus value. In Marxist writings, in other words, "exploitation" is a technical term.)

Historically there has been a long struggle over the length of the working day. Owners have an obvious interest in having their workers work as long as possible beyond the "necessary labor time," as this increases their production of surplus value. Workers, by contrast, have an interest in working as little beyond the "necessary labor time" as possible, since they are working for the benefit of someone else during this time. In the early nineteenth century it was normal to work 12, 14, or even 16 hours per day. In the United States, after much Labor agitation, the 8 hour working day was introduced on May 1, 1886. (The international celebration of May 1 as "Labor Day" has its origin in this historic event.)

THE ACCUMULATION OF SURPLUS VALUE: CAPITAL

The relations sketched out above are basically the same in a case where someone owns a shop which can accommodate 10 workers instead of one. The cost of the factors of production (labor power, machinery, raw materials, etc.) is, to be sure, multiplied by ten, but so is the value produced during the average work day. The owner pays $160 for wages, and $40 for the means of production, but the daily output has a value of $320. The important thing for the owner is that he can collect a surplus value of $120, instead of $12. It is evident that the owner is the better off the more workers he can accommodate. If he can hire 500 workers instead of 10, his surplus value would rise from $120 to $6000. Owners, therefore, have a strong motive for acquiring as large a plant (means of production) as possible.

A shop owner who collects a surplus of $120 a day has more than he or his family needs to live on. (The hypothetical situation is one in which a worker can live on $16 per day). The owner now has to confront the question of what to do with his surplus value. In societies where capitalism has not yet shaped the basic behavior of the culture, increased consumption is the most common course of action. Pre-capitalist aristocracies, *e.g.*, cultivated a lifestyle in which wealth was predominantly spent on such luxury items as palaces, festivities, or the arts. In capitalist cultures, by contrast, wealth is predominantly used to create more wealth, *i.e.*, it is invested in expanded production facilities which make possible the generation of an increase in surplus value. (This is the main reason why the old aristocracy in Europe was overwhelmed and pushed aside by the increasingly prosperous and powerful bourgeoisie.) Money or wealth in itself is not yet capital. "Capital" is by definition money (or wealth in the form of other assets) which is used to create more money. Thus, if the above shop owner has been acculturated into a capitalist society (or frame of mind), he will use his profits to acquire more means of production in order to accumulate still more surplus value.

A full fledged capitalist now, the owner is involved in an upward-bound spiral of investment and accumulation: The more means of production he acquires, the more workers he can hire. The more workers he hires, the more surplus value he will receive. And the more surplus value he receives, the more means of production he can afford to buy. The more he has, the more he can get.

It is important to notice that only owners of means of production (the "capitalists") have the possibility of being involved in this upward-bound spiral. People who do not own means of production, and who therefore have to sell their labor power to someone else (the "proletarians"), will essentially always just get what they need to live, and thus remain forever in their dependent position. During good times, and in individual industries, they may receive a little extra, *i.e.*, their "disposable income" may increase occasionally, but as a rule very few of them will ever get enough to acquire sufficient means of production themselves. (If too many workers earned enough to acquire means of production themselves, Capitalism would collapse. If most people worked for themselves, capitalists would simply not find the labor power which they need to operate their means of production.)

THE EXPANSION OF CAPITAL: MODERN INDUSTRY

What the individual capitalist does, is done by thousands of other capitalists as well. The general use of surplus value for the creation of more surplus value results in a multiplication of the means of production on a gigantic scale. In no epoch of human history has there been such an explosion of the number of productive facilities as in the period of capitalism. Capitalism has transformed the face of the earth more profoundly than any other type of civilization. It has, in fact, replaced the natural world by a man-made world. This can be seen in more detail by considering the development of the various factors of production:

1) The reinvestment of surplus value creates an ever increasing number of shops, factories, warehouses, roads, railroads, canals, ships, administrative centers, etc., i.e. the productive facilities and infrastructures needed for the production, transportation, distribution, sale and servicing of goods produced. Rural and wilderness areas are turned into industrial landscapes with the smokestacks, power lines, dumps, and associated mass housing developments which have become the most visible characteristics of industrialized nations.

2) Increased levels of production require ever greater quantities of raw materials and energy. Labor saving technology makes modern industry particularly energy dependent. These raw materials and fuels have to be wrested from the earth by mining, logging, drilling, dredging and other methods which have left highly visible scars on the landscape, or have damaged natural resources beyond repair.

3) Growing numbers of people are drawn to the growing centers of industry: industrialization is paralleled by urbanization. When rural areas are depopulated, older cultures vanish. Capitalist development has caused migrations of unprecedented proportions in many parts of the

world. It has restructured population distribution according
to industrial needs.

Capitalism is the most productive system that humanity has
ever known. The motivating force behind its productivity is
competition. In order to succeed, individual enterprises have
to compete for new markets while holding on to their old ones.
New markets are won by underselling competitors. In order
to sell more cheaply, products have to be produced more
cheaply. This means that more items of a certain kind have
to be produced in a given time with a given amount of labor,
or the same number of items in a shorter time or with less
labor. If a manufacturer succeeds in producing fifty pairs of
shoes in an hour instead of twenty pairs, he can afford to sell
his shoes at a lower price, thereby gaining a larger share of
sales in the marketplace.

Lower production costs can be achieved in two major
ways—both of which account for basic features of the modern
work world:

  1) By organizing the process of production as efficiently
as possible. One of the most important factors in this
organization is the division of labor, i.e., the division of
complex work processes into a number of simple ones which
can be performed mechanically, and at great speed. (Instead
of having a worker build a whole motor, which would require
knowledge, skill, and much time, managers have a number of
workers do just one thing—such as attaching a particular
part—which can be done with very little training or thought.)
The versatile and individually paced work of pre-industrial
craftsmen is replaced by the repetitive movements of the
modern assembly-line worker. At the same time, the many
performances of thousands of workers are coordinated in huge
assembly line plants and regimented by strict labor rules.

  2) By improving the means of production. This is
achieved in part by developing cheap raw materials (plastics,
for example), efficient energy (electricity), but primarily by
developing improved machinery. More scientific and
technological inventions have been made and used in the
period of Capitalism than in any other period of human

history. With suitable machines a few workers today can produce what formerly required a large workforce; large amounts of merchandise can be manufactured in a single day that formerly required weeks or months to produce. The unprecedented productivity of Capitalism is largely a result of the constant drive to improve technology.

In the long run, only those companies who can afford sophisticated machinery and large-scale production will stay competitive. Small and out-dated manufacturing companies will lose their market shares. Thus, mass production has come to dominate modern industry. The shoe factory replaces the independent shoe maker, the furniture factory the cabinet maker, the argribusiness the family farm, and the super-market the street corner store. Because the small producers cannot compete with large scale production, they eventually have to give up their independent business and seek employment with bigger companies, i.e., they become "proletarianized." It is primarily this development which has led to the breakup of traditional, small communities, and to the mass migration of people to urban, industrial areas.

Large scale production and sophisticated technology require large amounts of investment capital. Once a capitalist economy has reached a certain level of development, only investors with considerable amounts of money or credit can enter the competition. The owner of a small shop, no matter how clever and industrious, simply has no realistic chance of keeping pace with the development of big corporations, occasional exceptions notwithstanding. At the beginning of industrial capitalism, it was still possible for newcomers with limited resources to start new enterprises and succeed. Under conditions of advanced technological development, successful newcomers became increasingly rare. The more technology progresses, the more exclusive the class of capitalists.

This also sheds some light on the growing gap between the rich and the poor nations of the world. The rich nations are as a rule those who have the most sophisticated means of production, and who, therefore, can compete most successfully in the world market. As an independent shoe maker cannot compete with a shoe factory, a technologically underdeveloped nation cannot compete with a fully industrialized nation. And as the independent craftsman will eventually be forced to sell his labor power to a bigger company, the poor nation will be forced to give up its attempts to develop a competitive industry and sell the only thing it has — usually cheap raw materials, or primary agricultural products such as coffee, sugar, bananas, or cotton. As the proletarianized craftsman loses his independence, so does the economically weak nation: it has to produce what the rich nations need, and sell at prices which the entrepreneurs of the rich nations offer. This insures that, as a rule, the poor nations never succeed in accumulating enough surplus value to develop their own sophisticated industry. As long as they remain within a competitive market system, they are condemned to remain underdeveloped.

"Encouraging news, gentlemen! Our research department has come up with a moth that will eat synthetics!"

THE FORMATION OF MONOPOLY CAPITALISM

In a system of competition there are winners and losers. Since bigger companies have a better chance to produce cheaply than smaller ones, the bigger companies often drive their weaker competitors out of business, or induce them to "merge" with them before it is too late. Thus, in industry after industry, smaller companies vanish from the scene, and a few big corporations remain to dominate the field. Where formerly hundreds, if not thousands, of independent companies and entrepreneurs competed with each other for shares of the market, a handful of giants now administer, with little competition, what is left of the market. Although in the various industries there is usually more than one single corporation left, the remaining enterprises have a virtual monopoly over their domain. Competitive capitalism has transformed itself, by the very fact of its own competitiveness, into a system of monopoly capitalism.

This monopolization tends to do away with certain advantages that competitive capitalism has had for the consumer. Uncontrollable competition had forced entrepreneurs to sell their goods as cheaply as possible. Monopolistic corporations, because of their small number, can reach formal or informal agreements on prices, thus making price independent of such factors as supply, demand, or production cost. The results are artificially inflated prices — one of the major factors of general inflation in developed countries. The absence of competition also removes any incentive to improve the quality of products. Monopolistic corporations often have, in fact, good reasons to produce products of inferior quality. By producing tires or lightbulbs, for example, which wear out earlier than necessary from a technological point of view, corporations can force customers to buy more of their products, and thus make bigger profits.

Under monopoly capitalism, corporations have grown to such gigantic proportions that they can often openly challenge the power of national governments. When a particular government decides, *e.g.*, to raise corporate taxes, or to enforce environmental laws, a corporation can threaten to withdraw its capital from this particular country and invest it in some other, more "friendly" nation, leaving the original country with tens of thousands of workers suddenly unemployed. This power rivalry has since become a rather general problem, as many of the giant corporations have become "transnational." By spreading their assets over several countries or continents, and by shifting their assets around at their convenience, transnational corporations can easily evade control by those societies in which they conduct their operations.

In spite of numerous conflicts between governments and big business, it would be a mistake to conclude that big corporations could survive without the massive help and intervention of governments. While in the early days of industrial capitalism the state was to be restricted to providing a safe and legal framework for the operations of entrepreneurs and the functioning of the free market, in the time of monopoly capitalism the state has to provide its vital services to keep the economy in reasonably good health. This is most obvious when public funds have to be used to bail out failing corporations: society simply cannot allow tens of thousands of employees to lose their jobs because of the impending bankruptcy of a major corporation. · But the support of the state is also available to corporations in such matters as loan guarantees, negotiations with foreign countries, long-term planning, research, demographic statistics, training of a sophisticated workforce, repair of environmental damages, as well as their purchase of enormous quantities of military hardware and other goods that have kept many a company from economic collapse. The fact is that the old distinction between the public domain (the state) and the private sector (the economy) is not very clear cut anymore, and not always meaningfully applicable.   The viewpoints, interests, and influences of the major corporations reach deep into the organs of government, and governments are deeply involved in the operations of big business. Both domains form a single, intricate system. A system, however, which is committed to the continuing expansion and private accumulation of surplus value.

IMPERIALISM

Modern Imperialism is a system of international relations in which technologically underdeveloped nations become economically dependent on a small number of highly industrialized ones. To understand the dynamics of this system one simply has to examine what happens when a strong capitalist economy grows to such an extent that it becomes too big for the narrow confines of a nation state. It will help to look again at the development of the individual factors of production and distribution.

1) Investment Opportunities. A developed capitalist economy generates enormous amounts of surplus value. For this surplus value new, profitable investment opportunities have to be found. As long as a country is not yet fully industrialized, investment opportunities can be found at home. Eventually, however, a point will be reached when these opportunities are greatly diminished or even depleted. At this point, entrepreneurs will be forced to look beyond the boundaries of their home country. Overseas territories with their lack of modern production facilities are a welcome area for their activities. Thus, entrepreneurs "export their capital," i.e., they build mines, refineries, warehouses, ports, railroads and telecommunications systems in the underdeveloped parts of the world. (In this way Western civilization has been spread across this planet—often against the resistance of native populations who were not ready to part with their own ways of life.)

2) Raw Materials. Growing economies have growing needs for raw materials. At a certain point, raw material resources at home become insufficient or too expensive to extract. Increasingly, companies have to cover their needs with supplies from abroad. Some of these supplies are acquired by trade, i.e., bought from foreign countries. More typically, however, they are acquired by buying the sources themselves: Companies of developed nations became the outright owners of forests, plantations, mines, etc., in the less developed regions of the world. This is, as a rule, cheaper for

"Before we demand that our govenrment protect our
industry from cheap foreign imports made at slave-
labor wages, we have to deal with the fact that we own
sixty percent of those foreign plants."

the user of raw materials, and in addition coincides with the need to reinvest surplus value in new ventures. As a result the most profitable enterprises in underdeveloped countries are often owned by foreign companies, depriving the host country of badly needed revenues. In recent decades such countries have sometimes tried to nationalize such foreign holdings, arguing that the original investment capital of the foreign companies has usually been earned back many times over. But threats of severe reprisals, ranging from military occupation to the withholding of credit, have prompted most poor countries to refrain from implementing such designs.

3) Energy. Growing economies also have growing energy needs. This is particularly the case where human labor power is progressively replaced by machines: the less labor intensive an industry becomes, the more energy dependent it will usually be. Companies prefer to acquire their energy abroad in the same way that they acquire their raw materials: by owning the sources. Oil wells, refineries, and distribution facilities in the Mideast and Latin America, e.g., used to be almost exclusively owned by companies of industrialized nations, thus providing cheap energy for the developed countries, while still guaranteeing considerable profits to the oil companies. In the case of oil, however, the typical pattern of controlling foreign energy sources was eventually disrupted when most of the oil producing countries nationalized their energy assets and formed a cartel, thus allowing them to accumulate capital themselves, and to break out of the cycle of dependence and underdevelopment.

4) Markets. A growing economy needs expanding markets to dispose of all the goods which it produces. Although consumption in the developed nations has constantly increased, domestic markets are in the end insufficient to absorb the entire output of growing economies. Again, foreign countries in which investments are made are also a logical choice for the creation of new markets. As a result, the natives of these countries are increasingly inundated by the more "sophisticated" products of the industrialized nations, usually prompting them to abandon their own products, and, with them, their old way of life. Since fully industrialized nations produce comparable goods

"If we do not prevail upon our government to preserve democracy in those banana republics, we will have to present our stockholders with some dire news!"

more cheaply than the less developed industries of poor countries, these latter countries often fail to develop their own industries altogether, thus remaining in a state of permanent dependence.

5) Labor Power. More and more corporations discontinue parts of their operations at home and relocate their facilities in countries where labor power is considerably cheaper, due to lower standards of living. Such relocations create problems of unemployment in developed nations, but they seem to help less developed countries by furthering their industrialization, thus seemingly offsetting the tendency toward the permanent underdevelopment previously mentioned. The problem with this kind of industrialization, however, is the fact that most of the means of production are owned by the foreign corporations, and that therefore the generated surplus value flows back to the developed countries. The underdeveloped countries are simply used as reservoirs of inexpensive labor power. They are rarely enabled to accumulate the amounts of capital which are necessary to acquire the means of production which would allow them to use their labor power for their own benefit.

Historically, the penetration of overseas territories by technologically developed nations has taken different forms. In the nineteenth century it was normal to militarily occupy and politically annex such areas, i.e., to colonize them. This was mostly practiced by the European powers. In the twentieth century, such blatant forms of foreign domination became less and less acceptable. Thus, outright political control was replaced by economic control, a form of domination which is more subtle and less visible. It grants political independence to a country, but effectively regulates its policies by owning or controlling most of its means of production. The Montana based Anaconda Copper Company's ownership of Chile's major industry, copper mining, is an example. In recent decades even the ownership of means of production has become politically troublesome, and there has been a shift toward controlling poor nations primarily by controlling the flow of credit. Since most poor nations are heavily indebted to their wealthy creditors (often to the point of having to borrow more money simply to pay the interest on previous debts), they have effectively lost all freedom of movement.

This dependency on the rich nations is often a traumatic experience for the inhabitants of poor countries. They find themselves surrounded by means of production which they do not own, inundated by foreign products, controlled by appointees of absentee owners, and yet hopelessly caught in a vicious circle of underdevelopment and poverty. This situation would hardly have persisted for so long if it were not for the fact that the upper classes in these nations are usually staunch allies of the foreign powers. These upper classes use their dominant positions in their respective societies to keep things at status quo.

A typical situation in underdeveloped countries is that less than two percent of the population (the hereditary upper class) own more than eighty percent of the arable land. The majority of the mostly rural population has to eke out an existence on the remaining land. This explains why in countries which could produce an over-abundance of food stuffs, many people suffer from hunger or malnutrition. For the choice acreage owned by the upper classes is not used to grow the needed foodstuffs (as this would not be so profitable for them), but rather to grow cash crops which can be sold abroad. The revenue from these cash crops, furthermore, is not usually transferred back to the underdeveloped country, but rather deposited in the banks of the affluent nations (partly in anticipation of popular revolutions, which would expropriate the available tangible assets of the upper classes). In most of the poor nations, in other words, there is a small upper class which has its own reasons for resisting any social change. They would have been swept away by popular discontent long ago if they had not found a natural ally in foreign investors, who have helped them to stay in power by mobilizing the support of their own governments in the maintenance of the status quo in these underdeveloped nations.

The local upper classes traditionally control the state and its organs, particularly the legislative systems and the military. They use the security apparatus to maintain public order — an order which implies their privileged situation. They also use this apparatus to legalize and protect the holdings of foreign companies. In return, they are supported by the foreign governments who consider it their duty to protect the foreign holdings of their major corporations. The United States government, e.g., spends millions of dollars each year to train and equip armies in Latin America, armies whose only function is to keep their own restive populations in check. By keeping exploitative minority classes in power in poor nations, the rich nations can maintain a system which keeps the poor nations underdeveloped and dependent indefinitely.

"THE ULTIMATE CRISIS OF CAPITALISM"

According to Marx, capitalism has been the most productive and liberating system that humanity has ever known. Its expansionist dynamics (descriptively praised in the first chapter of the *Communist Manifesto*) have had the most profoundly revolutionary effect on the world. But capitalism is also a system which has its own eventual destruction built into its process. It is the very reason for its success which will in the end promote its downfall: its enormous productivity.

Competition drives capitalists to constantly improve their means of production, and thereby to increase their output. The problem is that the market does not grow at the same rate as productivity; capitalists tend to produce more than they can sell. While, technologically speaking, the developed capitalist economies could easily supply the rest of the world with an overabundance of goods, there will be proportionately ever fewer buyers who can afford to purchase this supply. Eventually the discrepancy between the capacity to produce and the capacity to consume will be so great that the capitalist system of production and distribution will begin to seriously malfunction, creating a crisis that may allow the possibility of the acceptance of an alternative system of economics.

Throughout the history of capitalism there have been cyclical crises of overproduction: Entrepreneurs have always produced as much as they could, eventually glutting the market. When consumers can no longer purchase all the goods that are offered, manufacturers cut back on their production, usually laying off part of their workforce. This leads to a reduction of the buying power of the pool of consumers, leading to a further reduction of production, further lay-offs, and so on. Eventually, however, recessions of this type have bottomed out, and production and consumption resumed at an even faster rate than before. The invention of new technologies and their corresponding industries (railroads, electrification, automobiles, etc.), as well as wars and the subsequent reconstruction of the devastated nations involved, have usually served as the stimulants for the rejuvenation of the economy. There are many who expect the "micro-chip revolution" to play a similar role in stimulating once more the vitality of the capitalist system, via the replacement of older, more obsolete technologies.

(It should be noted, incidentally, that overproduction is not measured against actual human needs, but against the capacity of people to buy. A glutted market can well exist side by side with great numbers of people who cannot buy even the bare necessities for survival. At present, large amounts of food are destroyed in the European Common Market, for example — at a time when fifteen to twenty million people in the "Third World" are dying annually as a result of starvation.)

The crisis of overproduction has been with the capitalist nations for many decades now; it has been hidden rather than resolved. It has been hidden by enlarging the market in a number of artificial ways. The growing advertisement industry tries frantically to persuade consumers to buy ever more goods, whether they need them or not. Planned obsolescence, the deliberate production of shoddy goods, insures that the market does not shrink. The export of often dubious products (infant formula for people who would be nutritionally better off breast-feeding their offspring, for example) to the "Third World" has the same effect. And one of the most important ways of saving productive capacities from idling is the production of expensive weapons systems which are sold to governments with their vast buying power. Without the massive armaments of the developed nations, capitalist economies almost everywhere would be in deep trouble. Yet, in spite of all these measures, a large percentage of the industrial capacities of developed nations are idling, and at present there are no sound prospects of new markets large enough to absorb everything which could be produced.

Whether the crisis of overproduction can be dealt with in one way or another within the the capitalist system, or whether it will eventually undo capitalism, is even debated among

Marxists.   Some argue that the eventual collapse of the
system is inevitable.   Others argue that Capitalism will only
be weakened by these internal contradictions, but that
determined revolutionary action is necessary to actually bring
about its downfall.   What Marxists agree on is that
Capitalism is besieged by the crisis of overproduction, and
that so far the crisis has been covered up rather than
resolved.

THE SOCIAL IMPLICATIONS OF
CAPITALISM

THE FORMATION OF SOCIAL CLASSES

Capitalism presupposes that only one part of a given population owns means of production, while the greater part does not. If most people owned their own shops, farms, or stores, industrial entrepreneurs would not have the labor force to operate *their* means of production. Historically, capitalism became possible only when there were sizable masses of dispossessed people who had to sell their labor power to owners of means of production to make a living. (This is one reason why capitalism was impossible during the early decades of the United States: as land was cheap and available to anyone, people preferred to work for themselves instead of selling their labor power. Only when land became scarce, and wave after wave of immigrants tried to make a living, did entrepreneurs find the labor pool which they needed. If Jefferson's idea of a republic of independent farmers had been realized, capitalism would have been impossible in the United States.)

Owners of means of production who have to buy labor power to operate them and who use their means for the creation of surplus value are "capitalists." Together with their necessary associates who help them with the management and administration of their assets (higher level managers, bankers, economists, lawyers, scientists, etc.) they constitute the class of the "bourgeoisie." Those who do not own means of production, and who therefore have to sell their labor power to make a living, are "proletarians." Together with other people engaged in productive activities (craftsmen, small farmers, etc.) they constitute the "working class." Some people (such as small shop owners, teachers, or prostitutes) do not easily fall into either category. On the whole, however, modern capitalist societies are characterized by the existence of two major classes, the one characterized by the ownership of the means of production, and the other one by non-ownership. The open or latent opposition between the two classes shapes much of the politics of modern nations.

Capitalists (or their managerial agents) organize the process of production, while the proletarians work under their direction. This obliges capitalists to have a sufficient level of understanding of the economic process, while workers (unless encouraged by unions to raise their standards of education) become easily uninformed, uninterested, or even demoralized. The bourgeoisie maintains certain levels of education for itself, thus enabling its members to wield power not only in the area of economics, but in the areas of politics, culture, and mass communications as well. In this way the bourgeoisie becomes a ruling class.

There have been other class societies before the emergence of Capitalism. In Greece and Rome of antiquity, a small class of freemen ruled over a mass of slaves, and during the Middle Ages, the mass of peasant serfs of Europe lived under the rule of their feudal lords. What is common to most class societies is the fact that a small upper class rules over and appropriates the surplus created by the lower class. What distinguishes them from each other is the form in which class rule and exploitation take place. The slave masters were legally entitled to the surplus labor of their slaves because they owned the slaves outright. The feudal lords were entitled to the surplus because they owned the land to which the serfs were attached by law. Capitalists are entitled to the surplus value produced by their workers because they own the means of production. It is usually the ruling class which creates the legal framework that justifies their continuing privileged position. Once such a framework has existed long enough, even the lower classes find it "natural" that some people are born into privileged positions, while others have to contend with a harder life.

In a capitalist society wealth is primarily used to create more wealth, i.e., surplus value is invested in such a way as to create more surplus value. This means that the wealth of capitalist societies expands much more rapidly than in other class societies. Since it is primarily the bourgeoisie that accumulates this expanding wealth, their position vis-a-vis the working class becomes ever more powerful; the distance between the two classes increases. While both classes have improved their standard of living in absolute terms during the last 150 years, in relative terms, the upper class has become considerably more wealthy than the working class during this period.

Paradoxically, this gap is today less visible than it was during the nineteenth century, when there were easily identifiable class cultures. Today the super-rich have become very discrete in their display of wealth, and in many cases a millionaire may dress, eat, and talk like a working man. To perceive relevant class distinctions in contemporary society often requires a high degree of analytical skill. Consequently, other social distinctions are much more often noticed than that between owners and non-owners of means of production: Black vs. White, Catholic vs. Protestant, Anglo vs. Chicano, Male vs. Female, Blue Collar vs. White Collar, etc. In times when the working class is under intensive pressure (in situations of job scarcity, for example), these distinctions often become an excuse for venting frustrations and feelings of hostility by a scapegoat mechanism which hides the real source of social antagonisms. When Black and White workers compete with each other for scarce jobs, they often end up hating each other because they are easily identifiable groups, rather than those who may be responsible for creating job scarcity. Marxist class analysis would hold that ultimately a Black and a White capitalist have more in common than a Black capitalist and a Black worker, even though the latter may have common cultural roots. And a male and female worker have generally also more in common than a female worker and her female boss, even though both must function in a male dominated society. Marxist analysis holds that ownership of the means of production is a more decisive source of power over other people than most other institutions.

"There was a time when you could buy an entire
election for the price of a primary today."

THE LEGAL FRAMEWORK OF CAPITALISM

Ownership of the means of production is the basis of the wealth and power of the bourgeoisie. Thus, wherever the bourgeoisie is in control of society, they will tend to create laws which provide a legal safeguard and justification for their holdings. Historically this has found expression in the constitutional provisions which make the right to own private property one of the most fundamental principles of modern societies — as fundamental as the right to life and liberty. Sometimes this right is even described as an "inalienable" right, *i.e.*, a right which supposedly existed in the state of nature, before any social or governmental organization. John Locke, the classic philosopher of this school of thought (and the theoretician of the first successful bourgeois revolution, the Glorious Revolution of 1688) wrote in his second *Treatise on Civil Government*: "The state of nature has a law to govern it, which obliges every one, and reason, which is that law, teaches all mankind, who will but consult it, that being all equal and independent, no one ought to harm another in his life, health, liberty, or possessions, . . ." The point of making the right to own private property one which exists before and independently of any social organization is to make sure that no rational society or government will take it upon itself to abridge or abolish that right. For legitimate social organizations are only those who enforce the rights given by nature. A government or society that would expropriate any individual property would thereby commit an unnatural act.

Theoreticians like Locke assumed that they were voicing the interests of all human beings. There is, however, a noteworthy peculiarity involved in treating the right to own private property as the same kind of right as that to life and liberty. For while every citizen has a natural interest in seeing his or her life and liberty protected, not every citizen may have an interests in the safeguard of his or other people's holdings. Everybody has a life and a certain amount of liberty, but not everybody has private property — particularly not extensive means of production.   In a society where a minority owns almost all the valuable land, for example, many citizens may be driven by sheer misery to conclude that such ownership should not be condoned or protected by social institutions.   Yet, once the right to own private property has been constitutionally declared inviolable, the resources of the state (police, judicial system, prisons, etc.) have to be committed to protect the holdings of the wealthy against the designs of the poor.   A bourgeois constitution provides the legal framework within which a minority can own and accumulate wealth without any interference on the part of the less fortunate; it is a framework which legalizes the exercise of power of the economically strong over the economically weak.   An alternative constitution may declare life and liberty inviolable, but stipulate that all means of production (as opposed to personal possessions such as clothing, books, furniture, family homes, etc.) are the common property of all citizens.   Such an alternative implies, of course, that rights concerning property are not "natural," but the expressed will of those who write constitutions.

Once the law has declared private property, particularly the private ownership of means of production, inviolable, social inequality has been made permanent — in spite of and because of the principle of equality before the law.   All citizens have a right to have their holdings protected by the security apparatus, but only owners derive an actual benefit from that provision: the law helps them to protect their privileged position.   All citizens have the right of free speech, i.e., to make their views known to society, but only those who own or can buy access to means of mass communication can make truly effective use of this right.   (Owners of means of communication will naturally give preference to views which support the right of their ownership.)   All citizens have the right to obtain legal counsel in a court of law, but only few have the means to pay for lawyers with sufficient resources to deliver effective services, which results in unequal treatment by the courts of the rich and the poor.   All citizens have the right to run for public office, but only those with access to wealth can afford to launch and carry out candidacy, and so forth.   As Anatole France once said: "The law forbids with equal majesty for the beggar as well as for the millionaire to sleep under the bridges."

CAPITAL EXPANSION AND LEISURE

Since the beginning of industrialization, capitalist entrepreneurs have been forced by competition to replace people with machines wherever they could: machines produce more goods more cheaply than human beings. Where formerly dozens of workers were necessary to produce a certain amount of goods, today one worker, with the help of a good machine, can produce at least the same amount, if not more, in the same time. The cost of the machine in the long run is lower than the cost of labor power, thus the entrepreneur with the best machines will be more competitive than the one who has to employ many workers to do the same job. All entrepreneurs have, therefore, a strong incentive to constantly modernize their equipment and either lay off workers or expand their production facilities. The general tendency in all areas of production is to invest increasing amounts of capital in machinery, and decreasing amounts in labor power. And this trend seems to be irreversible with the advent of the "micro-chip revolution" and the large-scale development and use of industrial robotics.

In the past the introduction of labor-saving machines did not result in a leisure society. People who were replaced by machines were by and large re-absorbed into the production process, either because the old industries increased their production, or because entirely new industries were created by new technologies. Capitalist societies, in other words, did not maintain their former production levels with less labor, but rather increased their output with the same, or even larger, labor force. Faced with the choice of more free time or more goods, the choice offered by improved technology, capitalist society opted for more goods. From a capitalist point of view this is, of course, a necessary choice: Surplus value is not to be consumed, but to be reinvested in better machines to create more consumer goods whose sale will in turn create more surplus value. The purpose of technology is not so much to make life more agreeable, but rather to gain an advantage in the permanent struggle of economic competition.

"Don't get me wrong, gentlemen. I don't *like* ten percent unemployment, but I can live with it."

The process of continuing reinvestment in improved means of production is not an economic problem as long as the expansion of the market is sufficient to absorb all the produced goods. At a certain point, however, the productive capacities will exceed the ability of people to buy everything which can be produced. At this point, entrepreneurs will not be able to absorb the part of the workforce which is replaced by the machines, and "structural unemployment" will become a permanent feature of advanced capitalist economies. Without an expanding economy, improved technology will translate into forced idleness on the part of many.

Two scenarios are imaginable in this situation. Either society will live with a large percentage of unemployed workers. (This has certain advantages for entrepreneurs: people who are afraid of being relegated to the "reserve army" of the unemployed tend to work harder and make fewer demands. But there is also a great potential for social unrest, as antagonistic groups of Blacks and Whites, men and women, etc. compete for increasingly scarce jobs.). Or society will divide the remaining work equitabley among all its members – thereby effecting a significant reduction of the average labor time. Once society produces enough for all of its members, technology need not be used anymore exclusively to increase output, but can also be used to increase the quantity and quality of leisure time.

"Gentlemen, we need to say something *positive* about *some* aspect of toxic waste."

CAPITAL EXPANSION AND THE ENVIRONMENT

In advanced capitalist countries industrialization has reached a point where further expansion may seriously threaten the environment in which people have to live. Every year more forests are cut down, more fields paved over, more rivers canalized or dammed up, more historical buildings and neighborhoods razed, and more landscapes and communities ruined by industrial waste dumps. The threats posed by industry are either direct (toxic waste which seeps into the ground water; air pollution; destruction of micro-organisms in the soil by over-fertilization; damaging noise levels around airports or helicopter landing sites; etc.) or indirect (the lack of accessible quiet areas for recreation; the transformation of the countryside into industrial wastelands or commmercial zones; the defacement of cities by expressway systems with their high noise and pollution levels; etc.) Life in urban areas has in recent decades become unpleasant in the short run, dangerous in the long run.

The reasons why a capitalist economy is almost inevitably driven toward the destruction of the environment are the same as those which drive capitalist enterprises beyond national borders to establish imperialist relationships with less developed nations: (1) The search for more raw materials and energy, (2) The search for new investment opportunities for their accumulated surplus and (3) The search for new market outlets. And increasingly there is (4) the need for inexpensive dump sites where the usually highly toxic by-products of modern industrial production can be deposited. The destruction of the environment, in other words, is not necessarily the result of individual greed or personal callousness on the part of the owners of industry, but a logical implication of a system which is based on the necessity to constantly expand, *i.e.*, to constantly reinvest surplus value in order to create more surplus value. The driving force behind industrial expansion is not so much human will as it is the inherent logic of the capitalist system.

This inherent logic, this self-driving force behind industrial expansion, also explains why even elected governments are relatively powerless to check the progress of environmental destruction. Since most governments implicitly accept the capitalist premise that most surplus has to be used to create more surplus, they are committed to maintain as best as possible a minimum of yearly economic growth. Economic growth implies a growth of the amount of goods and services, and therefore a need for growing amounts of raw materials and energy. Thus, while governments are also under the pressure of citizens to maintain a liveable environment, they are under the greater pressures of corporations to allow them to make further inroads into the environment. There is little chance to save the environment while Capital is allowed to expand indefinitely.

As governments are dragged along by the needs of capital, so are the labor unions. It has become almost commonplace today that wherever a forest has to be cut down to make room for a new airport, a bog dried up to allow the construction of a shopping mall, or an historic monument leveled to be replaced by an expressway, unions will side with the corporations against the environmentalists. Their motive is, of course, their desire to find jobs for their members. The problem is that in their thinking they have conceded the decisions as to how jobs are created entirely to the strategists of the corporations, instead of thinking of alternatives which in the long run would be more wholesome. It is by no means an unshakable dogma that a society can productivly work only if corporations are allowed to look for the most profitable investment opportunities. The preservation of the environment, e.g., could in many cases provide as many jobs as its destruction — even though this may not be as profitable for investors as other projects. But to see things in this manner would presuppose that one extricates oneself from the inherent logic of capital expansion, and that one bases policy decisions on other premises than the assumed necessity of creating more surplus value.

MONOPOLIES AND THE MEDIA

The tendencies which develop in a capitalist economy in general also assert themselves in the special case of the media. As the means of communication become technologically more sophisticated, they require more capital for their installation and operation. While earlier it was relatively easy to start, *e.g.*, a newspaper, today's high speed presses, mechanized news bureaus and well-staffed advertising departments require so much money that only big corporations or established "press czars" can afford to buy into the newspaper business. The inevitable result is that the multitude of small and independent papers either go out of business or are bought up by their big competitors. In the United States, *e.g.*, of the approximately 1700 papers which remain today, over half are owned by just twenty corporations. The monopolization of the news business progresses as fast as that of other industries.

What is true for the newspapers holds for other communications media as well: magazines, radio and television stations, the film industry, and the major textbook publishing houses are increasingly owned by a decreasing number of corporations. Ten corporations own over half of the radio market in the United States, eleven others half of the book market, and only four corporations publish most of the textbooks which are used in American schools today. Just three corporations (Columbia, Gulf & Western, and Universal MCA) produce over half of all prime time television shows. What sometimes deceives people about the media is the existence of hundreds of small presses and maverick companies which here and there produce prize-winning books or movies. In terms of market shares all these small companies are, however, negligible. The fact is that in the United States, approximately fifty corporations determine what the overwhelming majority of Americans read, see and hear.

"Well, we don't have to worry about the *Daily Blade*
badmouthing us any more. We just bought fifty-one
percent of their parent corporation."

Monopolization does not only take place within the individual media, but also across the entire communication industry. CBS, *e.g.*, does not only own an important part of the television market, but a good number of radio stations and publishing enterprises as well. And the communication industry does not operate independently of other industries, but is owned to a large extent by corporations which have nothing to do with book publishing or broadcasting. Thus, big banks and life insurance companies hold controlling shares in ABC, CBS, and RCA (the parent company of NBC). The First National Bank of Chicago owns controlling shares of Holt, Rhinehart, Winston, and all the stock of eighty daily newspapers. Members of the board of directors of The *New York Times* are also members of the boards of corporations as IBM, American Express, Bethlehem Steel, Morgan Guarantee Trust, Sun Oil, and several leading banks. The significance of this is that the same corporations which tend to control economic life in general also control the means of communication. The media are, therefore, not so much independent institutions (a "fourth estate"), which, through critical examination, counterbalance the power of the corporations, but rather an extension of these corporations. And if it is true that the big corporations are the backbone of a ruling class, then the media industry tends to be a tool in the hands of that class.

The control exercized by the owners of the media is usually not direct; the cases of explicit censorship in the United States are relatively rare. Control is rather exercised by choosing editors-in-chief, or chief executive officers whose views of the world coincide with those of the owners, and by promoting journalists who are least likely to risk their careers by producing controversial items. The net effect of this kind of control is not much less effective than that exercized by more official censors in other countries. The vast majority of readers, viewers, and listeners are treated to a fare of news, analyses, and entertainment which does not seriously criticize or scrutinize the power of those who control the means of production and communication. In large American newspapers, no overtly socialist column will ever appear besides those of conservative and liberal commentators, and no systematic critique of capitalism will ever be on prime time television, no matter how much the media profess to be impartial and open to a pluralism of opinions. The perimeters of public awareness are effectively set by those who have high stakes in preserving the status quo.

MARX'S THEORY OF ALIENATION

MARX'S THEORY OF ALIENATION

In his main work, *Capital*, Marx analyzes the actual dynamics of the capitalist system: the creation of surplus value, the reinvestment of surplus value, its accumulation, the development of modern technology, etc. *Capital* is to a large extent a book on economics. It is significantly distinguished, however, from the usual writings in economics by the fact that it also investigates the social and historical implications of economic developments. Marx's work is essentially interdisciplinary; it cannot be adequately understood within the confines of isolated academic disciplines.

Certain aspects of Marx's analysis of capitalism are philosophical. One of the basic concepts which Marx took from the philosophical tradition is Hegel's notion of Alienation. In Hegel's largely idealistic philosophy the active human mind "alienates" itself by creating an external, objective reality of the spirit (in the form of moral and legal systems, works of art, bodies of knowledge, etc.) which in time develops a life of its own, not only independently of its creators, but also reacting back to and shaping the active minds of humanity. The objective world of the spirit, culture, is made by minds, but in turn also creates these minds. The product tends to control the producer.

Marx conceived of his own version of the theory of Alienation by applying Hegel's notion to the world of material production. In his thinking it is not only the human mind which creates an external reality, but human beings in their entirety. Human labor, physical as well as mental, is engaged in creating a man-made world which increasingly replaces the natural world, and which surrounds its makers in ever more noticeable ways. Alienation in Marx's thinking is a situation in which the products of human labor are separated from the human beings who create them and assume control over the lives of their makers, eventually alienating humans from themselves and their humanity. It is a situation which Marx's contemporary, Thoreau, has expressed in such formulations as: "We are not riding on the railroad, it rides on us" and "But lo! men have become the tools of their tools" (*Walden*). And it is a tendency in human civilization which today finds expression in such science fiction visions as the story of man-made computers or robots that cut themselves loose from their makers to control or threaten them.

Marx developed his theory of Alienation in a series of somewhat sketchy notes which he took while reading such classical economists as Adam Smith and David Ricardo. The notes were not discovered until the twentieth century, and then published as *Economic and Philosophical Manuscripts of 1844*. In these notes Marx distinguishes between four main aspects of alienation:

a. *The Alienation of the Worker From the Product of his Work*

The worker (the modern work force) replaces at an increasing rate the natural world by a man-made world, thus seemingly fulfilling the old dream of complete human control over the forces of nature. Yet, since workers usually do not own what they produce, the man-made world confronts them as something alien, as something which they do not control or even understand. Instead, this alien world increasingly controls every aspect of the lives of its makers. The market, *e.g.*, is a human institution which is made, maintained, and supplied by the collective effort of working people. Yet, people find themselves more and more at the mercy of market forces which affect their lives profoundly, but which are entirely beyond their control. Their situation is determind by price fluctuations, inflation, joblessness, gluts, etc., but they control these forces as little as their ancestors controlled such forces of nature as floods, droughts, or blights. The alienation of workers from the world which they produce is particularly striking in the case of the production of modern weapons systems: scientists, engineers, designers, white collar workers, blue collar workers, secretaries, administrators, etc., all participate in the production of means of annihilation which periodically victimize their makers, and which threaten the very existence of the makers without their understanding how and why. Humanity, instead of controlling nature, is controlled by its own products.

b. *The Alienation of the Worker From the Process of Production.*

In modern industry workers do not work anymore under their own direction (as, for example, the independent craftsmen in pre-capitalist societies), but under the supervision of managers who are in charge of planning and coordinating the process of production. To increase output, managements divide complex work processes into simple, repetitive tasks which workers have to perform in machine-like fashion. The rhythm of work is determined by the quasi-military discipline of the factory, and by the requirements of the machines to which the workers are assigned. In this way, the very activity of the workers is taken away from them; in their productive activity they are essentially passive.

(This aspect of modern industrial work is brilliantly satirized in Charlie Chaplin's *Modern Times.* Time and again this movie reveals the violence which is done by the industrial mode of production to individuals who are not yet dulled enough to perform like robots. The aspect of the worker's passivity in his activity is epitomized in the episode where even the activity of eating is taken out of the hands of the worker and assumed by a feeding machine which subjects the worker to its predetermined rhythm.)

c. *The Alienation of the Worker From Human Nature.*

The essence of human nature, according to Marx, is free, conscious activity. Modern industrial production, however, is neither free nor conscious. Workers are driven to work by external necessities, and their activities are as little guided by deliberation as those of ants or bees. In fact, the whole process of capitalist production is not an expression of human choices and designs, but is directed by forces beyond human control. In a capitalist economy, production does not serve human beings, rather human beings serve production. People do not work in order to live, they live in order to achieve ever higher levels of production. Human beings, with their original freedom and intelligence, become mere means in a process of economic growth which has become an end in itself.

d. *The Alienation of Workers From Each Other.*

As workers tend to become mere appendices of machines, or obedient tools in the hands of managers, they also fail to relate to each other as human beings. Instead of cooperating freely and intelligently with each other in the determination of their common fate, they become a "mass" in the pejorative sense, a passive collective in which autonomous individuals are transformed into anonymous entities. As workers conceive of themselves as mere means of production, they also think of others in this way. They are estranged from other workers to the extent that they are estranged from themselves and their humanity.

~

The abolition of alienation is to be achieved by people taking possession and control of the man-made world which they have produced, and which they maintain by their labor. In terms of Marx's economic analysis, working people are to be the owners of the means of production, thereby enabling them to accumulate any surplus value themselves, and to reinvest or consume it as they themselves see fit. The assets of industrialized societies are not to be used anymore to further a process of expanding production unrelated to real human needs, but to allow people to develop the potential which is usually smothered by drudgery and mindless consumption.

In political democracies only the state is subjected to democratic control, while the economy is in the hands of a relatively small number of industrial leaders. Since economic might is as much a power as the might of the state (and in its effects on the daily lives of people, often even more pervasive than state power), an economic system controlled by a minority of industrial leaders is in conflict with the idea of self-government. The point of a social democracy is to subject not only the state, but also the economy to democratic control. The self-determination of people is threatened not only by dictatorial governments, but also by the uncontrolled power of big business. If the idea of self-government is to be furthered, political democracy has to be extended to become a social democracy.

The highest value in Marx's thinking is not affluent material consumption, but self-determination. Even if the socialization of the means of production were to imply a reduction of production and consumption, the measure would still be worth it in terms of the ability of people to determine their own fate. This perspective was summarized programmatically by Friedrich Engels in his *Socialism: Utopian and Scientific*: "With the seizing of the means of production by society the mastery of the product over the producer is done away with. . . . Then for the first time, man, in a certain sense, is finally marked off from the rest of the animal kingdom, and emerges from mere animal conditions of existence into really human ones . . . Only from that time will man himself, more and more consciously, make his own history . . . It is the ascent of man from the realm of necessity to the realm of freedom."

NOTE ON READINGS

The following works by Marx and Engels are short, easily understandable, and most useful as an introduction to Marxist thought.

1. Karl Marx: *Value, Price, and Profit*

    (A clear summary of the main ideas of Marx's Capital, written for British trade unionists.)

2. Friedrich Engels: *Socialism: Utopian and Scientific*

    (A very popular summary of the basic thoughts of Marxism.)

3. Karl Marx: *The Civil War in France*

    (An account of the Paris Commune of 1871, and its bloody repression by government troops. This book gives a concrete illustration of the political and historical dimensions of Marxist thought.)

4. Karl Marx: *The Economic and Philosophical Manuscripts of 1844*

    (These relatively difficult notes provide insight into what may be called the "philosophical foundations" of Marx's critique of capitalism. The sections on "Alienated Labor" and "Private Property and Communism" are most important.)

Any further reading should start with volume I of *Capital*, Marx's main work. Its analysis of the capitalist mode of production is extensive, but, after the initial discussion of the concept of value, easy to read and filled with a wealth of material concerning the early history of capitalism.

The development of Capitalism in the twentieth century is

characterized by two major phenomena: Monopolization and Imperialism. No work on these phenomena has yet gained the status of a classic in the way *Capital* has, but an early popular account of Imperialism is V.I. Lenin's *Imperialism, The Highest Stage of Capitalism*, and a somewhat more scholarly account of Monopolization (with a special focus on the U.S.A.) is P. Baran's and P. Sweezy's *Monopoly Capital*. A more recent investigation of contemporary Imperialism is H. Magdoff's *The Age of Imperialism*.

SELF-DETERMINATION
An Anthology of Philosophy and Poetry
Edited by Jorn K. Bramann

A new, interdisciplinary approach to the modern concept of 'self' through the eyes of the great philosophers, writers and poets of Europe and America, from Descartes to Nietzsche, with powerful new translations. "This collection should be especially useful in stimulating student thought — just right for classroom use. The interesting juxtaposition of different strands of philosophic thought centered on one theme, and a meaningful one at that, strikes me as being a valuable educational tool. And I especially liked the intermingling of excerpts from poets, novelists, and social thinkers as well as philosophers." **(Harry Magdoff, co-editor of *Monthly Review*).**
$10.95, 256 pp. illustrated ISBN 0-913623-00-8

ADLER PUBLISHING COMPANY
P.O. BOX 9342
ROCHESTER, NY 14604

OTHER BOOKS FROM ADLER

THE PEACEABLE KINGDOM, By Peter Wild. A new collection of poems by one of America's most respected poets and 1973 Pulitzer Prize nominee. Inspired by the American primitive paintings of Edward Hicks, Wild's poems suggest the imminent reversion to base nature in the illusions and delusions of the 'American Dream.' "Peter Wild has mastered the art of writing out of a completely personal world while giving the illusion that he is working with an exterior reality. This wonderful contradiction creates a kind of wholeness of perception that is rare in any poetry. It is a poetry of first the eye, then the ear, and finally the mind" (**Diane Wakoski**)
$6.95, 64 pp., illus.   ISBN 0-913623-01-6
(26 Signed, Numbered Ltd. Ed., $15.00)

ANOTHER STORY, By Brian Swann. A new novella from a master of the school of experimental fiction. Brimming with realistic details of life in the English countryside and in New York City, a raunchy surrealism invests the protagonist with a kind of purpose as he travels through his time warp, trying to remain sane. "For Brian Swann, an 'absurdist' writer who actually is one, story comes out of nothing and goes back into nothing. What is left is a residue of voice. Swann's is unique in contemporary fiction: startling, comic, cutting, spare" (**Robert Coover**).
$7.95, 128 pp.   ISBN 0-913623-03-2
(26 Signed and Numbered Ltd. Ed. $25.00)

UNEMPLOYMENT AND SOCIAL VALUES: A collection of Literay and Philosophical Texts. Issue Number 4 of *Nightsun,* interdisciplinary journal of philosophy and literature. As European prime ministers, presidents and labor leaders wrestle with the concept of a shorter work week and the centenary of the eight-hour work day approaches (May 1, 1886), this timely issue addresses the reduction of labor, environmental destruction and material consumption, as well as self-realization instead of full employment. Poetry by Al MacDougall, Jeff Poniewaz and Antler, short stories by Jochen Ziem and Gerald Haslam, an interview with Michael Harrington on Leisure and Unemployment and more.
$6.95, 96 pp.   ISSN 0278-6079   ISBN 0-913623-02-4

ADLER PUBLISHING COMPANY
P.O. BOX 9342
ROCHESTER, NY 14604

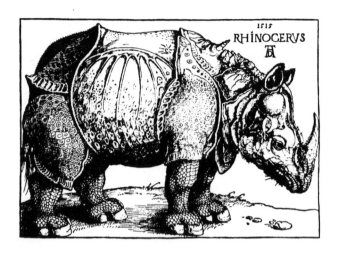

FORTHCOMING BOOKS FROM ADLER

UPRISING IN EAST GERMANY and Other Stories, By Jochen Ziem.
First English book-length translation. Ten powerful short stories from
the East German author who went to West Berlin to become "One of the
few writers of international stature that Germany has produced since
Hacks, Grass, and Johnson" (*Times Literary Supplement*).
$8.95   ISBN 0-913623-07-5

**WITTGENSTEIN'S TRACTATUS AND THE MODERN ARTS, By
Jorn K. Bramann.** A goundbreaking study of the structural similarities
between the early classic of Analytic Philosophy and the art, literature,
poetry, cinema and architecture of the twentieth century.
$15.95   ISBN 0-913623-05-9

ADLER PUBLISHING COMPANY
P.O. BOX 9342
ROCHESTER, NY 14604